Shadows in Plain Sight

Unveiling the Bystander Effect in the Psychology of Help

Freudian Trips

Copyright Page

Disclaimer

The views and opinions expressed in this book are those of the author(s) and do not necessarily reflect the official policy or position of any other agency, organization, employer, or company. The contents of this book are for informational and educational purposes only and are not intended to serve as professional advice, diagnosis, or treatment.

The information provided in this book is believed to be accurate and reliable as of the date of publication. However, it may include some errors or inaccuracies, and no warranty or guarantee is provided regarding the accuracy, timeliness, or applicability of the content.

Readers are encouraged to consult with professional philosophers, educators, or other qualified professionals where appropriate for personalized advice. The author(s) and publisher shall not be liable for any loss, damage, or harm caused or alleged to be caused, directly or indirectly, by the information or ideas contained, suggested, or referenced in this book.

Chapter 1: Introduction to the Bystander Effect

Understanding the Bystander Effect

Imagine walking down a busy street and seeing someone trip and fall. You look around and notice that everyone else is merely observing or walking past. You might feel the urge to help, but there's a strange pull that stops you—maybe it's the thought, "If no one else is helping, why should I?" This phenomenon, where individuals are less likely to offer help to a victim when other people are present, is known as the Bystander Effect.

Historical Context: A Shocking Event Sparks Inquiry

The concept of the Bystander Effect became widely discussed following a tragic event in 1964. In New York, a young woman named Kitty Genovese was attacked near her home. Reports suggested that numerous neighbors heard or witnessed the attack but did not come to her aid or call the police. This shocking incident raised questions: Why did no one help? Was this inaction a common response in emergencies?

Pioneering Research: Latané and Darley's Experiments

To answer these questions, psychologists John Darley and Bibb Latané began exploring what happens when people witness emergencies. They conducted a series of experiments in the late 1960s and early 1970s. One famous experiment involved participants sitting in a room filling out a questionnaire. Suddenly, smoke began to fill the room. When a participant was alone, they quickly reported the smoke. However, when they were in the room with others who seemed unconcerned, they were much less likely to react or seek help. This and other experiments by Darley and Latané helped establish the Bystander Effect as a significant psychological phenomenon.

Diffusion of Responsibility: A Key Factor

A critical concept introduced by these studies is diffusion of responsibility. This idea suggests that when we're in a group, we don't feel as compelled to act because we assume someone else will. So, in the case of Kitty Genovese, each neighbor might have thought, "Surely, someone else will call the police."

Overview of the Book Structure and Objectives

This book aims to delve deep into the Bystander Effect, exploring its psychological underpinnings, societal impacts, and ways to overcome it. We'll look at how culture, media, and technology influence this phenomenon, and how understanding it can lead to more compassionate and active communities.

In upcoming chapters, we'll explore how our actions are influenced by those around us and the internal conflict between self-preservation and the moral urge to help.

We'll discuss real-life cases, from everyday incidents to landmark events, examining the role of bystanders in each.

Finally, we'll explore strategies to counteract the Bystander Effect, empowering readers to become proactive helpers in their communities.

A Journey of Understanding and Action

As we embark on this journey, remember that the Bystander Effect is not about assigning blame. It's about understanding human behavior and our inherent social nature. By learning about this phenomenon, we can begin to recognize these moments in our own lives and feel more prepared to break the cycle of inaction. Let's step into this exploration with open minds and a willingness to see the world, and ourselves, a little differently.

Chapter 2: Psychological Foundations

Navigating the Human Mind in Groups

When we're with others, our behavior often changes, sometimes in ways we don't even realize. This chapter explores how being in a group influences our actions, especially when it comes to helping others—or not.

The Power of the Group: A Psychological Perspective

Imagine you're at a concert, and everyone starts clapping. Even if you didn't enjoy the performance much, you might find yourself clapping along. This simple example shows how groups can sway our actions. When we're in a group, we're not just individuals; we're part of a collective that subtly guides our behavior.

Social Influence: The Invisible Hand

Social influence is like an invisible hand that shapes our decisions. It comes in many forms:

Conformity: This is when we change our behavior to match others around us. Have you ever agreed with a friend's opinion, even if you didn't fully believe it, just to avoid standing out? That's conformity in action.

Peer Pressure: It's not just a term for teenagers. Peer pressure affects all ages. It's the direct or indirect push we feel from others to behave in a certain way.

Social Norms: These are the unwritten rules of behavior in a society. For example, standing in line is a social norm; we do it because it's an accepted way of maintaining order.

Diffusion of Responsibility: Why We Step Back in Groups

Now, let's talk about why we might not help someone when we're in a group. This is where the concept of diffusion of responsibility comes in. It's a bit like being in a team project at work. If you're alone on a project, you know it's all on you. But in a team, you might think, "Someone else will handle this part."

When we're in a group witnessing someone in need of help, a similar thought process occurs. We think, "There are so many of us here, someone else will surely step in." This belief that others will or should take action can lead to a paradox where no one does anything.

Understanding Our Own Psychology in Groups

To understand why we act (or don't act) in groups, we need to:

Recognize Social Influence: Be aware of how others' behavior affects ours. Next time you're in a group, try to notice if you're doing something just because others are.

Reflect on Our Decisions: Ask yourself, "Am I not acting because I truly believe I shouldn't, or is it because I think someone else will?"

Be Mindful of Social Norms: Sometimes, these norms can prevent us from helping. Challenge them by thinking, "What's the right thing to do here, regardless of what everyone else is doing?"

Empowering Ourselves to Act

Understanding the psychology behind our behavior in groups can empower us to act more independently and helpfully. It's about recognizing the unseen forces that influence us and choosing to respond not just as part of a group, but as compassionate individuals.

In the next chapters, we'll explore how these concepts play out in different cultural settings and how empathy and moral reasoning can influence our decisions to help others. Remember, understanding our psychology isn't about judgment; it's about gaining the insight to make better choices, both as individuals and as part of a larger community.

Chapter 3: Societal and Cultural Perspectives

Culture's Lens on the Bystander Effect

Every society has its unique way of seeing the world, and these perspectives deeply influence how we behave, especially in group situations. This chapter explores how different cultures shape the way we respond (or don't respond) in situations where someone needs help.

Culture and Its Influence on Our Actions

Culture is like a set of glasses through which we see the world. It shapes our values, beliefs, and behaviors. For instance, in some cultures, community and collective responsibility are highly valued. In these societies, people might be more inclined to help others, even strangers. In contrast, in cultures that value individualism and personal responsibility, people might be less likely to intervene, thinking that it's not their place or responsibility.

Comparing Bystander Behavior Across the World

Now, let's travel around the globe to understand how bystander behavior varies:

Collectivist Societies (e.g., Japan, China): Here, people often see themselves as part of a larger group. In emergencies, this might translate to a stronger communal response, as helping is seen as a collective responsibility.

Individualistic Societies (e.g., United States, United Kingdom): In these cultures, the emphasis is on individual autonomy. This can lead to a higher incidence of the Bystander Effect, as people might assume someone else will take responsibility.

Social Norms and Expectations: The Unseen Guides:

Social norms and expectations are like the unspoken rules of society. They tell us what's considered acceptable or unacceptable behavior. These norms can significantly influence whether we decide to help someone in need.

Conformity to Norms: If a society's norm is to not get involved in others' affairs, people might hesitate to help, even in emergencies.

Fear of Misjudgment: Sometimes, people don't act because they're afraid of being judged or misunderstood. For example, they might worry about offending someone by offering help.

Expectation of Reciprocity: In some cultures, there's an expectation that a good deed should be reciprocated. This belief can either motivate people to help (hoping to receive help in return one day) or discourage them (if they believe the person can't reciprocate).

Understanding Our Cultural Conditioning:

To understand and potentially overcome the Bystander Effect, we need to be aware of our cultural conditioning:

Recognize Cultural Biases: Start by acknowledging the cultural norms that might be influencing your behavior.

Question the Norms: Ask yourself, "Is this norm helpful or harmful in emergency situations? Should I follow it or break it?"

Embrace Universal Empathy: Regardless of cultural norms, cultivating empathy can motivate us to help others. Empathy transcends cultural boundaries.

The Way Forward: A Cultural Mosaic of Help

As our world becomes more interconnected, we're exposed to a variety of cultural perspectives. This diversity can be a strength, allowing us to learn from each other and create a mosaic of helping behaviors. By understanding how our culture shapes our responses, we can become more conscious and active participants in our global community.

In the following chapters, we will delve deeper into the roles of empathy, morality, and self-preservation in the Bystander Effect, and how these elements interact with our cultural conditioning. Remember, the goal is not to judge but to understand and use that understanding to foster a world where helping each other becomes a universal norm.

Chapter 4: The Role of Empathy and Morality

Empathy and Morality: The Heart and Mind of Helping

Have you ever felt a tug at your heart when seeing someone in trouble? That's empathy at work. And when you think, "It's the right thing to help," that's your moral reasoning speaking. This chapter explores how these powerful forces within us can drive us to help others, overcoming the Bystander Effect.

Empathy: Feeling What Others Feel

Empathy is our ability to understand and share the feelings of another person. It's like putting yourself in someone else's shoes. When we see someone in distress, our empathy can make us feel a bit of their pain, sadness, or fear. This emotional connection can be a strong motivator to help.

Empathy in Action: Imagine you see a child lost in a mall, looking scared. Your empathy might make you feel their fear and prompt you to help them find their parents.

Moral Reasoning: Deciding What's Right

Moral reasoning is about thinking through what's right or wrong in a situation. It's our inner moral compass guiding us. This reasoning often draws from our values, beliefs, and societal norms.

Morality at Play: In the lost child scenario, your moral reasoning might remind you that helping lost children is the right thing to do, reinforcing your decision to help.

Altruism and Prosocial Behavior: The Science of Kindness

Psychologists use terms like altruism and prosocial behavior to describe actions done to benefit others. Altruism is helping without expecting anything in return. Prosocial behavior is any action intended to help others.

Altruism Explained: If you help the lost child without any thought of reward or recognition, that's altruism.

Prosocial Behavior in Everyday Life: Holding the door for someone or donating to charity are examples of prosocial behavior.

Case Studies: When Empathy Breaks the Bystander Effect

Let's look at real-life examples where empathy and morality triumphed over the Bystander Effect:

The Subway Hero: In 2007, Wesley Autrey, a construction worker in New York, saw a man fall onto subway tracks. Without hesitation, he jumped down and shielded the man with his body as a train passed over them. His quick, empathetic action saved the man's life.

The Lunchroom Incident: A high school student saw a classmate choking in the cafeteria. While others froze, she remembered her first-aid training and performed the Heimlich maneuver, dislodging the food stuck in her classmate's throat.

Fostering Empathy and Moral Courage

How can we cultivate empathy and moral courage in our lives? Here are some ways:

Practice Perspective-Taking: Try to understand situations from others' viewpoints. This builds empathy.

Reflect on Values: Think about your values and how they guide your actions. This strengthens moral reasoning.

Learn from Examples: Stories of people who have helped others can inspire us to do the same.

Small Acts Matter: Start with small acts of kindness. They can have a big impact and prepare you to act in bigger situations.

Conclusion: A More Empathetic and Moral World

Empathy and morality are powerful tools against the Bystander Effect. By nurturing these qualities in ourselves, we can create a more caring and responsive world. As we move forward, remember that each act of kindness, no matter how small, contributes to a culture of helping and moral courage. In the next chapters, we'll explore how fear, risk, and self-preservation play into our decisions to help or not, and how we can balance these with our empathetic and moral instincts.

Chapter 5: Fear, Risk, and Self-Preservation

Understanding Our Instincts in the Face of Danger:

When we witness a situation that requires intervention, like someone being harassed or an accident, our instinctive reactions play a significant role in our decision to act or not. This chapter explores the complex interplay of fear, perceived risk, and the instinct for self-preservation, and how they affect our response as bystanders.

The Power of Fear and Perceived Risk:

Fear is a primal emotion, and it's closely linked to our perception of risk. When we're in a potentially dangerous situation, our brain rapidly assesses the level of threat. This assessment can lead to a fight, flight, or freeze response:

Fight: Confronting the danger.

Flight: Escaping the situation.

Freeze: Being paralyzed by fear.

In bystander scenarios, fear and risk assessment can lead to hesitation or inaction. For example, if you see someone being attacked, the fear of getting hurt yourself might prevent you from intervening.

Self-Preservation vs. Moral Urges

Self-preservation is our instinct to protect ourselves from harm. It's a powerful force and often comes into conflict with our moral urges to help others. This conflict can create a mental tug-of-war:

On one side, there's the voice saying, "Help them, it's the right thing to do."

On the other side, there's a voice warning, "But what if you get hurt?"

Balancing these two can be challenging. Often, the instinct for self-preservation is stronger, as it's hard-wired into our survival mechanisms.

The Aftermath: Psychological Impact on Bystanders

Witnessing a traumatic event, even as a bystander, can have a lasting psychological impact. Feelings of guilt, shame, or regret are common if we feel we could have helped but didn't. This emotional aftermath can lead to:

Stress and Anxiety: Constantly replaying the event in your mind, wondering "What if?"

Helplessness: Feeling powerless because you didn't act.

Social Withdrawal: Avoiding situations that remind you of the event.

Coping with the Aftermath

Dealing with these emotions requires self-compassion and understanding. Here are some strategies to help cope:

Talk About It: Discussing the event with a trusted person can help process your feelings.

Reflect on Decisions: Understand that fear and self-preservation are natural responses. Reflecting on your actions can help you prepare for future situations.

Seek Professional Help: If feelings of guilt or anxiety persist, consider speaking to a counselor or psychologist.

Empowering Ourselves to Overcome Fear

While fear and self-preservation are natural, we can take steps to empower ourselves:

Knowledge is Power: Learning basic first aid, self-defense, or conflict resolution skills can boost your confidence to act.

Mental Rehearsal: Imagine different scenarios and think about how you could respond. This mental preparation can help in real situations.

Build Awareness: Being more aware of your surroundings can help you assess situations more accurately and reduce unfounded fears.

Conclusion: Finding Balance in Our Response

Understanding the role of fear, risk, and self-preservation helps us navigate the complex decision-making process in emergencies. By acknowledging these factors and working to balance them with our moral urges, we can become more effective and compassionate bystanders. In the next chapters, we'll explore the influence of media and technology on the Bystander Effect and how awareness and training can help us overcome these innate challenges.

Chapter 6: Media Influence and the Digital Age

The Digital Mirror: Reflecting and Shaping Our Responses

In today's world, media and technology are like a mirror reflecting and shaping our society. From news reports to social media, the digital age has transformed how we witness and respond to events around us. This chapter delves into how these powerful tools affect the Bystander Effect and our behavior as digital citizens.

Media and Technology: Amplifying or Muting Our Responses

Media and technology can have a dual role in influencing bystander behavior:

Amplifying Response: Sometimes, media coverage of a crisis or event can spur people into action. Seeing the suffering of others on our screens can trigger empathy and a desire to help.

Muting Response: On the flip side, constant exposure to distressing news can lead to desensitization. We might start feeling that these events are just 'normal' and not something extraordinary that requires our intervention.

Digital Disengagement: The Online Bystander

The phenomenon of digital disengagement occurs when people, despite being connected online, remain passive in situations that would typically call for help or intervention. This can happen for several reasons:

Overload of Information: The sheer volume of information and stories we encounter online can be overwhelming, making it hard to engage deeply with any one issue.

Lack of Personal Connection: Online, the personal connection to a situation or individual is often weaker. We might feel less compelled to act because it feels less real or immediate.

Anonymity and Distance: Being behind a screen can create a sense of detachment and anonymity, reducing the pressure to conform to social norms of helping.

Case Studies: When Viral Goes Vital

Let's explore some real-life examples where media and technology played a significant role in bystander behavior:

The Livestream Rescue: In 2017, a teenager livestreamed a distressing situation. Viewers of the livestream quickly alerted authorities, leading to a timely intervention. This case shows how technology can facilitate rapid response and mobilize help.

The Social Media Outcry: A video showing a social injustice went viral, leading to widespread public outcry and demands for change. This incident highlights how social media can amplify issues and galvanize collective action.

The Hashtag Movement: In response to a global crisis, a hashtag trended worldwide, raising awareness and funds. This movement demonstrates the power of digital solidarity and the ability of social media to unite people for a cause.

Navigating the Digital Landscape: Our Role as Digital Bystanders

In the digital age, being an active bystander also means being responsible and engaged online. Here are some ways to do this:

Stay Informed but Not Overwhelmed: Choose reliable news sources and limit exposure to avoid desensitization.

Engage Actively: Use social media to spread awareness about issues and ways to help.

Verify Before Sharing: In the age of misinformation, it's crucial to verify the authenticity of information before sharing it.

Conclusion: Harnessing Digital Power for Good

The digital age has undoubtedly transformed the way we view and respond to the world around us. By understanding the impact of media and technology on our behavior as bystanders, we can harness these tools to become more empathetic, informed, and active participants in our global community. In the next chapters, we will explore the legal and ethical considerations related to bystander intervention and how we can overcome the Bystander Effect through awareness and education.

Chapter 7: Legal and Ethical Considerations

Navigating the Crossroads of Law and Morality

When faced with a situation where someone needs help, we don't just consider our feelings or safety. We also think about the legal and ethical implications of our actions. This chapter explores the laws and ethical dilemmas related to the Bystander Effect and how they influence our decisions to act or not act.

Good Samaritan Laws: Protection for the Helping Hand

Good Samaritan laws are designed to protect people who offer help in emergency situations. These laws vary from place to place, but they generally share a common goal: to encourage people to help others without fear of legal repercussions, as long as they act reasonably and without negligence.

Example: Imagine you see a car accident and offer first aid to the injured. Good Samaritan laws are meant to protect you from being sued if the person you're helping claims your actions caused them harm, provided you acted sensibly and without intent to harm.

Ethical Dilemmas in Bystander Intervention

Ethical dilemmas arise when we're unsure about the right course of action due to conflicting values or principles. Here are some common dilemmas related to bystander intervention:

Risk vs. Responsibility: If intervening in a situation puts you at risk, what's more important – your safety or helping someone in need?

Privacy vs. Assistance: If helping someone means invading their privacy or autonomy, should you still intervene?

Misinterpretation of Situations: What if you misinterpret a situation and intervene unnecessarily, causing embarrassment or harm?

Legal Obligation vs. Personal Judgment

While laws provide a framework for what we can or cannot do, they don't cover every possible situation. Often, we have to rely on our personal judgment.

Legal Obligation: In some places, there are laws that require you to help in certain situations, like reporting a crime. Failing to do so could have legal consequences.

Personal Judgment: In scenarios not clearly defined by law, we rely on our judgment. This can be influenced by our values, experiences, and understanding of the situation.

The Balance Between Law and Morality

Finding a balance between legal obligations and personal judgment is key. Here are some guidelines:

Know the Basics of the Law: Familiarize yourself with the Good Samaritan laws and duty-to-assist laws in your area.

Consider Safety: Assess the safety of the situation. Helping doesn't mean putting yourself in harm's way.

Ethical Decision-Making: Reflect on what you believe is morally right. Sometimes, the legal and ethical paths might diverge.

Seek Guidance: If you're unsure, seek advice from legal or ethical experts, especially in complex situations.

Conclusion: A Compass for Action

Understanding the legal and ethical aspects of bystander intervention equips us with a compass for action. It's about finding the right balance between following the law, ensuring personal and others' safety, and acting according to our moral principles. As we move to the next chapters, we will explore strategies to overcome the Bystander Effect and how we can train ourselves to respond more effectively in situations that call for our intervention.

Chapter 8: Overcoming the Bystander Effect

Breaking the Cycle of Inaction

While the Bystander Effect is a common social phenomenon, it's not an unchangeable part of who we are. There are effective strategies and educational approaches that can help us counteract this tendency. This chapter focuses on how we can become more proactive in helping others, overcoming the hurdles that often hold us back.

Strategies to Counter the Bystander Effect

To move from passive observers to active helpers, consider these strategies:

Increased Awareness: Understanding the Bystander Effect is the first step. When we're aware of this tendency, we're better equipped to recognize it in real-time and overcome it.

Recognizing the Power of One: Remember that every individual has the power to make a difference. Realizing that your action, no matter how small, can have a significant impact, might encourage you to take the first step.

Building a Sense of Responsibility: Cultivate a sense of personal responsibility. If you see something happening, think, "If not me, then who?"

Educational Approaches to Promote Helping Behaviors

Education plays a crucial role in empowering people to overcome the Bystander Effect. This can be achieved through:

Training Programs: Workshops and seminars on first aid, conflict resolution, and emergency response can prepare individuals to act confidently in various situations.

Role-Playing Exercises: Practicing scenarios where intervention is needed can help people rehearse how they might respond in real life, reducing hesitation when a real situation arises.

Awareness Campaigns: Public campaigns can highlight the importance of bystander intervention and provide practical tips on how to act in different situations.

The Role of Training and Awareness

Training and awareness not only equip individuals with the necessary skills but also foster a mindset of readiness and responsibility. For example, CPR training doesn't just teach the technical skill; it also prepares individuals mentally to step up in a medical emergency.

Examples of Successful Interventions

Let's look at some instances where training and awareness led to positive outcomes:

The Alert Commuter: A commuter trained in emergency response used his skills to help a person who had a seizure on a train, providing immediate care until medical professionals arrived.

The Prepared Neighbors: Residents of a neighborhood attended a community safety workshop. When a fire broke out in one of the homes, these trained neighbors quickly organized a response, ensuring everyone's safety and minimizing damage.

Encouraging a Culture of Intervention

Creating a culture that encourages intervention is crucial. This can be fostered through:

Community Engagement: Involving community members in safety and awareness programs.

Positive Reinforcement: Publicly recognizing and praising individuals who act as responsible bystanders.

Policy Support: Encouraging organizations and governments to create policies that support and protect those who intervene to help others.

Conclusion: A Call to Action

Overcoming the Bystander Effect is about transforming our mindset from passive to active, from isolated to connected. By educating ourselves, practicing intervention skills, and fostering a culture of responsibility, we can all contribute to a more caring and responsive society. In the final chapters, we will explore case studies and interviews that provide real-world insights into overcoming the Bystander Effect and conclude with reflections on our role in a collective society.

Chapter 9: Case Studies and Hypothetical Interviews

Learning from Stories

The Bystander Effect is not just a concept studied in psychology labs; it's a real-world phenomenon with tangible consequences and inspiring examples of overcoming it. In this chapter, we delve into case studies and interviews with experts and everyday heroes who have broken the cycle of inaction.

Case Study 1: The Subway Rescue

Background: In a crowded subway station, a man suddenly fell onto the tracks. Amidst the shock and confusion, one bystander jumped down and pulled the man to safety just seconds before a train arrived.

Analysis: This incident highlights the power of decisive action in a crisis. The rescuer, despite the risk to himself, acted swiftly, influenced by a strong sense of responsibility and courage.

Lessons Learned: The importance of immediate response in emergencies and the potential impact of one person's action.

Case Study 2: The Neighborhood Watch Success

Background: A neighborhood, once plagued by petty crimes, transformed when residents started a neighborhood watch program. They worked together to monitor and report suspicious activities, significantly reducing crime rates.

Analysis: This case shows the effectiveness of community collaboration. By sharing responsibility and staying vigilant, the residents overcame the Bystander Effect collectively.

Lessons Learned: The power of community involvement and proactive measures in ensuring safety and security.

Hypothetical Interviews with Experts and Heroes

Interview with a Psychologist:

Topics Discussed: The psychology behind the Bystander Effect, strategies for overcoming it, and the role of societal influences.

Key Insights: Awareness and education are crucial in empowering individuals to act. The expert also emphasizes the importance of understanding our innate responses to emergency situations.

Interview with a Sociologist:

Topics Discussed: The impact of social dynamics and cultural norms on bystander behavior.

Key Insights: Social structures and norms can either inhibit or encourage helping behaviors. Changing these norms is a gradual process that requires collective effort.

Interview with an Everyday Hero:

Experience Shared: An individual recounts their experience of intervening in a public harassment incident.

Reflections: The interviewee talks about the initial hesitation, the moral conflict, and the eventual decision to intervene, driven by a sense of justice and empathy.

Breaking Down the Situations

Each case study and interview is accompanied by a discussion that breaks down the key factors at play:

Motivations for Acting: Understanding what drives people to step up in critical moments.

Challenges Faced: Analyzing the hurdles and fears encountered and how they were overcome.

Impact of Intervention: Reflecting on the outcomes of these actions, both on the individuals involved and the wider community.

Conclusion: Real Stories, Real Impact

These case studies and interviews provide not just insights but also inspiration. They show us that overcoming the Bystander Effect is not only possible but can lead to profoundly positive outcomes. By learning from these examples, we can better understand how to act effectively and compassionately in our own lives. In the final chapter, we will summarize the key insights from the book and explore future directions for research and action in understanding and mitigating the Bystander Effect.

Chapter 10: Conclusion and Future Directions

Reflecting on Our Journey

As we reach the conclusion of our exploration into the Bystander Effect, it's time to reflect on the key insights and lessons learned, and to consider the future directions for research and action. This chapter aims to consolidate our understanding and inspire continued efforts towards positive change in individual and collective behaviors.

Summarizing Key Insights and Lessons

Understanding the Bystander Effect: We've learned that the Bystander Effect is a psychological phenomenon where people are less likely to help in emergencies when others are present. It's influenced by factors like fear, social influence, and diffused responsibility.

The Role of Empathy and Morality: Empathy and moral reasoning are powerful motivators for overcoming the Bystander

Effect. Understanding and cultivating these qualities can propel us to act in critical moments.

Impact of Culture and Society: Our actions are deeply influenced by cultural norms and societal expectations. Recognizing and challenging these norms can help mitigate the Bystander Effect.

Legal and Ethical Considerations: The decision to intervene is often influenced by legal and ethical considerations. Understanding these factors can guide us in making informed decisions in complex situations.

Power of Individual Action: Each case study and interview emphasized that individual actions, no matter how small, can have a significant impact on others and the community.

Future Research Directions

Looking forward, there are several areas where further research could deepen our understanding and effectiveness in combating the Bystander Effect:

Technological Influence: Exploring how emerging technologies, like social media and virtual reality, impact bystander behaviors and developing strategies to use these platforms positively.

Cross-Cultural Studies: More research in diverse cultural contexts can provide a broader understanding of how different societies experience and respond to the Bystander Effect.

Long-Term Interventions: Investigating the long-term effectiveness of educational and training programs in changing bystander behaviors.

Psychological Resilience: Understanding how to build psychological resilience can help individuals better cope with the emotional consequences of intervening in distressing situations.

Final Reflections: The Role of the Individual in a Collective Society

As individuals in a collective society, our actions or inactions in critical moments can shape the world we live in. We are part of a larger community, and our responses to emergencies reflect and influence the values and norms of this community. By choosing to act, to be empathetic, and to take responsibility, we contribute to a more caring and responsive society.

A Call to Action

This journey through the Bystander Effect is not just an academic exercise; it's a call to action. Every one of us has the potential to make a difference. By staying informed, prepared, and empathetic, we can break the cycle of inaction. Let's carry forward the lessons learned and strive to be proactive bystanders, not just for ourselves, but for the betterment of our collective society.

In closing, the Bystander Effect challenges us to be more than just observers in life. It invites us to engage, to care, and to act. As we move forward, let's embrace this challenge and work towards a world where stepping up to help becomes the norm, not the exception.

About Freudian Trips

Welcome to Freudian Trips, your dedicated platform for diving deep into the world of psychology. We are more than just a YouTube channel or a book publisher. We are a beacon of enlightenment, making complex psychological concepts accessible and engaging for all.

Our YouTube channel is a rich repository of psychology made simple. We take the profound and often complex ideas from the world of psychology and break them down into digestible, easy-to-understand content. From the foundational theories of Freud to the cognitive insights of Piaget, we cover a broad spectrum of psychological schools and thoughts, making psychology accessible to everyone, regardless of their background or prior knowledge.

As a book publisher, we take the same approach, transforming intricate psychological theories into comprehensible narratives. Our books are not just collections of words, but vessels of wisdom that make psychology approachable and relatable. We believe that psychology should not be confined to academic circles, but should be available to all who seek to understand the human mind and behavior.

At Freudian Trips, we believe in the power of curiosity and the pursuit of knowledge. We are here to stoke the fires of your curiosity, to guide you on your intellectual journey, and to help you navigate the fascinating world of psychology.

If you are someone who is not afraid to question, to explore, and to learn, then you are in the right place. Join us on this journey of exploration, as we make psychology easy to understand, one concept at a time.

Be sure to visit our Youtube channel at: www.freudiantrips.com/youtube

You can also visit us on the web at www.freudiantrips.com

Welcome to The Freudian Trip community. Stay curious. Stay enlightened.